Good (morning, afternoon, evening) ladies and gentlemen, I am _____, your First Flight Attendant (today, this evening). On behalf of _____, I would like to welcome you on board Flight _____ (non stop to _____, terminating in _____ with intermediate stops at _____).

A Safety Information Card is located in the seat pocket in front of you. Because each airline and aircraft is different, we suggest that you review the card while the Flight Attendants demonstrate the safety features of this aircraft.

To most passengers,
their stewardess *is*
National Airlines. So we
are looking for young
ladies who have a flair
for making people happy,
young ladies with just
the right blend of
friendliness, competence
and poise. If you like
to travel, to meet people,
and to make them glad
you are going their
way, read on.

Stewardess

COME FLY WITH ME!

Elissa Stein

CHRONICLE BOOKS
SAN FRANCISCO

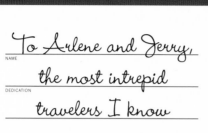

To Arlene and Jerry,
NAME

the most intrepid
DEDICATION

travelers I know

Page 111 constitutes a continuation of the copy-
right page. Every effort has been made to trace
ownership of all copyrighted material included in
this volume. Any errors that may have occurred
are inadvertent and will be corrected in subse-
quent editions, provided notification is sent to the
publisher.

Library of Congress Cataloging-in-Publication
Data available.

ISBN-10: 0-8118-5223-7
ISBN-13: 978-0-8118-5223-4

Manufactured in China

Designed by Benjamin Shaykin

Distributed in Canada by Raincoast Books
9050 Shaughnessy Street
Vancouver, British Columbia V6P 6E5

10 9 8 7 6 5 4 3 2 1

Chronicle Books LLC
85 Second Street
San Francisco, California 94105
www.chroniclebooks.com

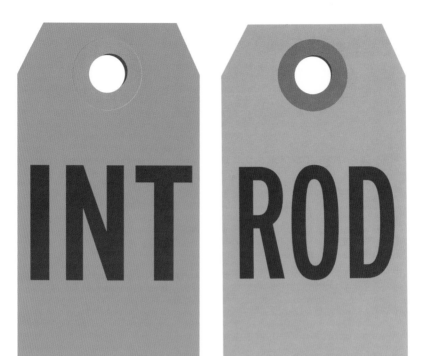

INTRODUCTION

"Now boarding Flight 23 to Miami."

With this announcement, the terminal is abuzz. Excited travelers gather packages and freshen up—straightening ties and grabbing briefcases, smoothing skirts and applying a new coat of lipstick. The passengers want to look their best as they approach the sunny stewardess waiting at the gate.

Hearts beat faster as she welcomes you aboard. In her crisp uniform and snow-white gloves, her pillbox hat perfectly perched atop that neat hairdo, she embodies both competence and glamour. With a gracious smile, she escorts passengers to their seats. And soon everyone settles in, thrilled at the very thought of flying.

"Ladies and gentlemen, please fasten your seatbelts."

And with those words, the adventure truly begins.

During the golden age of flying, when air travel was exclusive and thrilling and glamorous, a plane flight was anything but ordinary. People dressed to the nines to travel. Airports crackled with energy and activity and the lure of exotic locales. Planes had themed piano bars and cocktail lounges on board. Passengers on flights with sleeping compartments were served breakfast in bed. Seats were designed to swivel, so passengers could face each other to dine. Seven-course meals were served on fine china, atop freshly pressed linen. And stewardesses epitomized the experience—their designer uniforms, their perfectly coiffed hair, and their inviting smiles and welcoming manner inspired dreams of a life in the sky.

The very first air travel, though, was far from glamorous. Starting in 1918, airplanes were used to deliver mail, and only occasionally would a brave passenger or two venture on board. Back then, air travel was an impractical and risky venture. Weather conditions forced emergency landings in cornfields, and most landing strips were not equipped with lights, preventing night flying. By comparison, train travel was comfortable, reliable, and safe. But in 1927, Charles Lindbergh's transatlantic flight created public intrigue and presented air travel as the exciting future of transportation.

Then, in 1930, Ellen Church changed the face of flying. She approached Boeing Air Transport (which became United Airlines) with a radical new idea—why not have nurses on board to assist with the passengers? Boeing recognized the brilliance of this vision, and soon Ellen, a nurse herself, and seven others became the first stewardesses in the air. Other airlines followed, and soon women were an integral part of flight crews. Dressed in military-style uniforms, they served food and beverages, soothed nervous passengers, loaded luggage, helped refuel the plane, and even nailed down passengers' wicker chairs to the plane's floor when necessary. As the roles of stewardesses evolved, airlines created stewardess courses and schools to standardize training.

Although the first stewardesses were required to be nurses, after the start of World War II, when nurses were needed by the military, airlines opened their doors to the general population. So many thousands of women clamored for the chance of a career in the sky that admission to stewardess school was next to impossible. And for the lucky few who were hired by airlines, the rules they were bound to after graduation were rigorous—girdles and heels on every flight, strict height and weight restrictions, rigid hair and makeup rules, mandatory retirement at a certain age—generally between 27 and 32—and, to many the most difficult, forced grounding upon marriage. But the thrill of travel and the chance to escape conventional careers kept the competition to become a stewardess intense.

Airline executives quickly realized that having lovely and capable young women on board was a tremendous selling feature. As many people still

preferred train to air travel, airlines sought to personalize flying with friendly stewardesses and ever more luxurious service, with stewardesses promoted as the smiling face of the airlines. As the flight industry grew, stewardesses helped each airline establish its own distinct identity, with their glamorous images (rather than the pilots) featured on airline timetables and in advertisements.

Flying was expensive, and airlines catered to their customers. And with bigger planes, top-notch service, fine dining on board, and cocktails galore, passengers were loyal to their favorite airlines. But as competition for passengers increased, airlines scrambled to set themselves apart from all the others. They hired world-famous designers to clothe their stewardesses. Fashion shows debuting each new line were media events. Terminals got grander, lounges more luxurious. Five-star restaurants created elaborate in-flight dining choices.

In the 1960s, with the sexual revolution in the air, uniforms went from smart and tailored to sassy and revealing. In vibrant colors, vivid patterns, and clingy fabrics, microminis and go-go boots were all the rage. Everything got shorter and tighter. Advertising followed suit, with slogans such as "I'm Cheryl, Come Fly Me" and "We Would Move Our Tails for You." Much to the chagrin of many stewardesses themselves, they went from being professional career girls to sex symbols.

But while airline fashion and advertising moved in one direction, the forces of social equality moved in the other. In 1964, the U.S. federal government passed the Civil Rights Act, which held that employees could not be discriminated against because of age, race, or sex. And in 1971, federal courts found that airlines could no longer refuse to hire males to work on board as stewards. Stewardesses became flight attendants, men joined cabin flight crews, and uniforms got longer, blander, and more professional. Fashion trends in the air saw fishnets and hot pants replaced by navy blue, beige, or burgundy pantsuits. Stewardesses fought for, and won, equal pay; the right to retire when they wanted; and the right to fly when married, when pregnant, with natural hair color, with glasses, and with a few extra pounds. The women's rights movement found a place in the sky.

Along with new fashions and expanded rights, the 1970s also ushered in a fuel crisis. Massive jumbo jets with upstairs piano bars and passenger lounges were no longer profitable. And fare deregulation had airlines scrambling to keep prices competitive. Suddenly, everyone could afford to fly. Air travel lost its sense of luxury and glamour and became all about low fares and indistinguishable service. Once an exclusive adventure, flying became commonplace.

Although the flights featuring afternoon tea service, hand-carved chateaubriand, and glamour galore are long gone, the women who served us so well, with enthusiasm, dedication, and seemingly little effort, deserve recognition and celebration.

Welcome aboard.

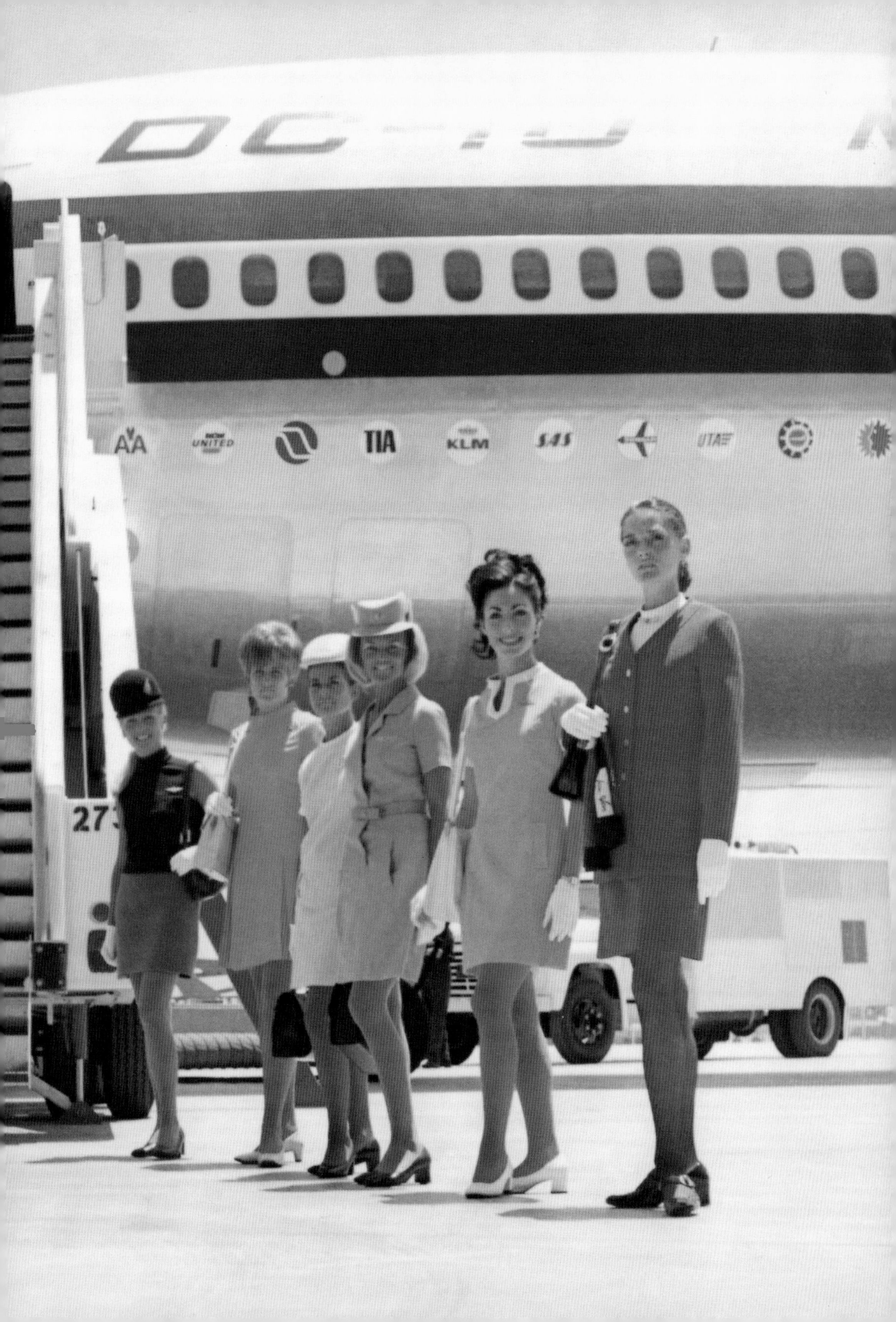
DC
AA
UNITED
TIA
KLM
SAS
UTA
27

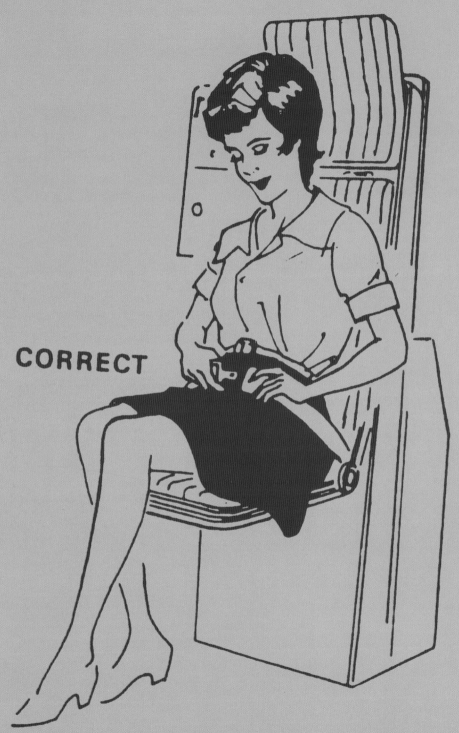

CORRECT

DC-10 FLIGHT ATTENDANT JUMP SEAT

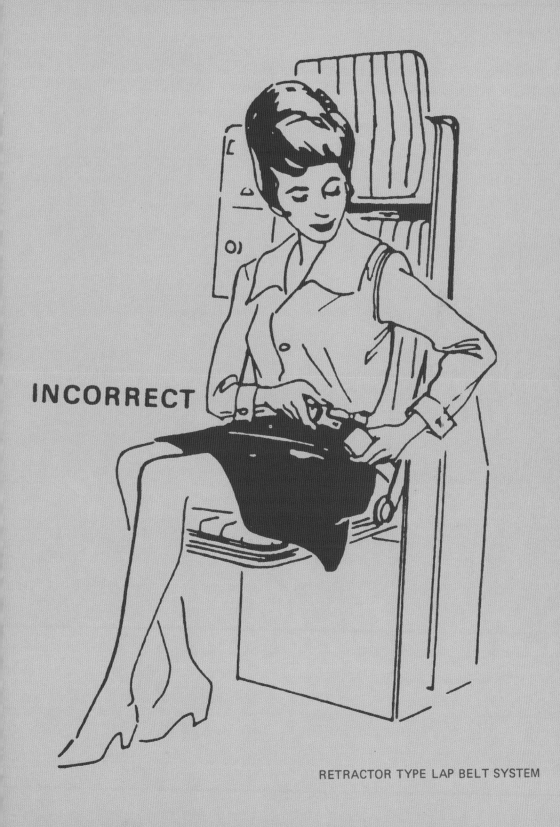

INCORRECT

RETRACTOR TYPE LAP BELT SYSTEM

Stewardess School

Not just anyone could be a stewardess. Each major airline had its own training program, and competition for a place in stewardess school was tough. To the lucky few who were accepted, training was a rigorous endeavor, with classes in food service, emergency procedures, airplane construction, the physics of flying, grooming, and deportment. But to those who made it through to have their uniforms custom fitted and their wings pinned on at graduation, the life of a stewardess held the promise of a dream come true.

Vicki, on hair

Many of us wore wigs or falls to ensure perfect hair. Falls were a nice way to keep hair tidy—they looked like a bob or a flip and would blend in with our bangs. Sometimes wigs were easier, as we had regulation hair colors and hairstyles to conform to. They'd get awfully hot on those ten- to fourteen-hour international flights, but our hair always looked just right.

Kay, on her lifelong dream

When I was eight years old, I saw a movie about a stewardess on her first flight. I remember that she forgot to check the catering, and the flight took off with no food. The pilot heard what happened and returned to the airport to pick up provisions for the passengers. All these years later, I can still remember the scene and the way the cabin and galley looked. That day I said that my goal was to become a stewardess.

Suzanne's favorite uniform

I loved the uniform I graduated in. It was a beautiful black dress with a jacket, a white hat, a black winter coat with a white scarf and white gloves, and, most important . . . wings that said *stewardess.* Soon after that, uniforms got shorter and sexier, but this was the height of elegance.

Judy's favorite memory

On a layover, the entire crew spent the night at Mount Fuji, in Japan. We were the only Westerners in the small town, and the local people were completely captivated by everything we did. They gave us kimonos to wear and laughed and laughed watching us trying to figure out how to wear them. I was so touched by their delight in welcoming us.

Rosanne's most embarrassing moment

Once, after a flight, I mistakenly gave one of the gentleman passengers the captain's jacket from the coatrack. The captain searched the entire plane for his jacket before I realized what I had done. I confessed my mistake, and the captain had to walk through the terminal in shirtsleeves. He didn't talk to me for a long time after that.

Pat, on being a stewardess

Flight attendants share a unique station in the history of aviation. We experienced a working life different than what had been before. We saw the best of the world of aviation, and we lived every inch of it, mile for mile.

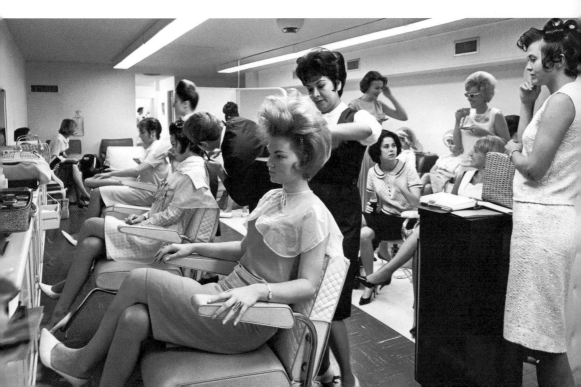

A classroom with a full-scale mock-up

of a plane instead of a blackboard.

Fine Dining at 30,000 Feet

(selections from a TWA in-flight menu, 1970s)

Appetizers from the Cart

FRESH IRANIAN SEVRUGA CAVIAR

ASSORTED HORS D'OEUVRE

Entree Selections

*Wherever We Fly, We Have the Enviable Opportunity to Taste
and Savor the Cuisines of Each Land. You are Invited to
Share Some of Our All Time Favorites.*

CHATEAUBRIAND ROTI
*A Roasted Double Tenderloin of Beef. Said to be created by Montmireil,
Personal Chef to Vicomte Chateaubriand, the Great French Writer and
Statesman of the Napoleonic Era. Complemented by Sauce Bearnaise.*

FILLETS OF SOLE WITH CRAB MEAT
*Poached North Atlantic Sole with a Crab Meat filling…
enhanced by a Creamy Herb and White Wine Sauce.*

CHICKEN CURRY
*Boneless Breast of Chicken in a Mild Curry Sauce.
Presented with Parslied Rice and a Selection of Sambals
such as Shredded Coconut, Raisins, Peanuts and Mango Chutney
to accent the Curry Flavor.*

INDIVIDUAL LAMB RIB ROAST
*A Specially Selected French Rack of Spring Lamb
Cooked to the Pink…A TWA Favorite!*

LOIN OF PORK COUNTRY STYLE
*Slices of Roasted Pork Loin are served in a Pan Gravy
with Savory Apple Stuffing.*

Salad

GARDEN SALAD BOWL

*An Array of
Fresh Garden Greens Consisting of Romaine and
Boston Lettuce, Endive, Red Cabbage and Shredded
Carrots, Tossed with an Assortment of Special Garnitures.
Your Choice of Roquefort, Creamy French,
or our Mustard Garlic Dressing.*

Desserts

BANANA SPLIT

*An all-time Soda Fountain Favorite!
Vanilla, Chocolate and Strawberry Ice Cream,
topped with your choice of Pineapple or Chocolate Syrup,
Sliced Bananas, Whipped Topping and Chopped Nuts.*

ON THE CHEESE BOARD
A Variety of Fine Cheeses of the World.

FRESH FRUIT IN SEASON

Amaretti Cookies   Dinner Mint

After Dinner Coffees

COFFEE FLAVORS OF THE WORLD
*The Perfect Touch of Hot Coffee and Whipped Cream.
It's the Spirit that Makes the Difference!*

JAMAICAN COFFEE   **CAFE ROYALE**   **CAFE PARISIENNE**
With Tia Maria   Coffee and Cognac   With Grand Marnier

ROMAN COFFEE   **CAFE MILANO**
With Tia Maria and Galliano   With Amaretto di Saronno and Rum

JAPAN AIR LINES

NOW
3 DELIGHTFUL
WAYS TO
THE ORIENT

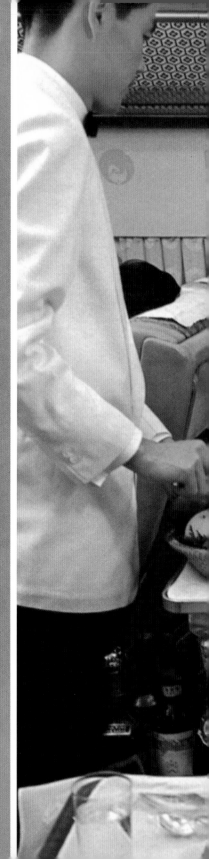

ONE REASON WHY AMERICAN SERVES YOU BETTER WHEN YOU FLY

"Here's America's   firs

No wonder American Airlines has the best trained stewardesses in the air

"This new million dollar stewardess college in Texas is a shining example of the special emphasis that American Airlines places on serving *you*, the passenger. It's the only college in the country entirely devoted to the training of airline stewardesses.

"Step inside. Everywhere you see signs of American's advanced training methods. The most modern visual aids! Complete mockups of aircraft! Courses that range from radio navigation to public speaking. 650 talented girls a year will receive training here that can't be duplicated elsewhere in the world. The first graduates are already serving you.

"American Airlines has always been famous for the best trained stewardess corps in the air. With this new college, American is making certain you will continue to enjoy that special blend of hospitality and efficiency you have come to expect on the Flagship Fleet."

nd only Stewardess College"

AA AMERICAN AIRLINES

America's Leading Airline

A Braniff International hostess is a
interest in people for themselves
security to the confused; a friend
a heroine to little girls; a source o

beautiful person. She is alive for her
She is a daughter to the middle aged;
o everyone who boards her plane;
oride and joy to her parents.

She has the ability to communicate
with the people with whom she comes

She knows how to serve meals and about aerodynamics, a lot about first aid,

beverages in a gracious manner, a little and even how to deliver a baby—just in case.

She is a model in how to walk, talk, sit, stand
is full of common sense about situations tha

pply make-up properly, and style her hair. She
ight occur in flight and on the ground.

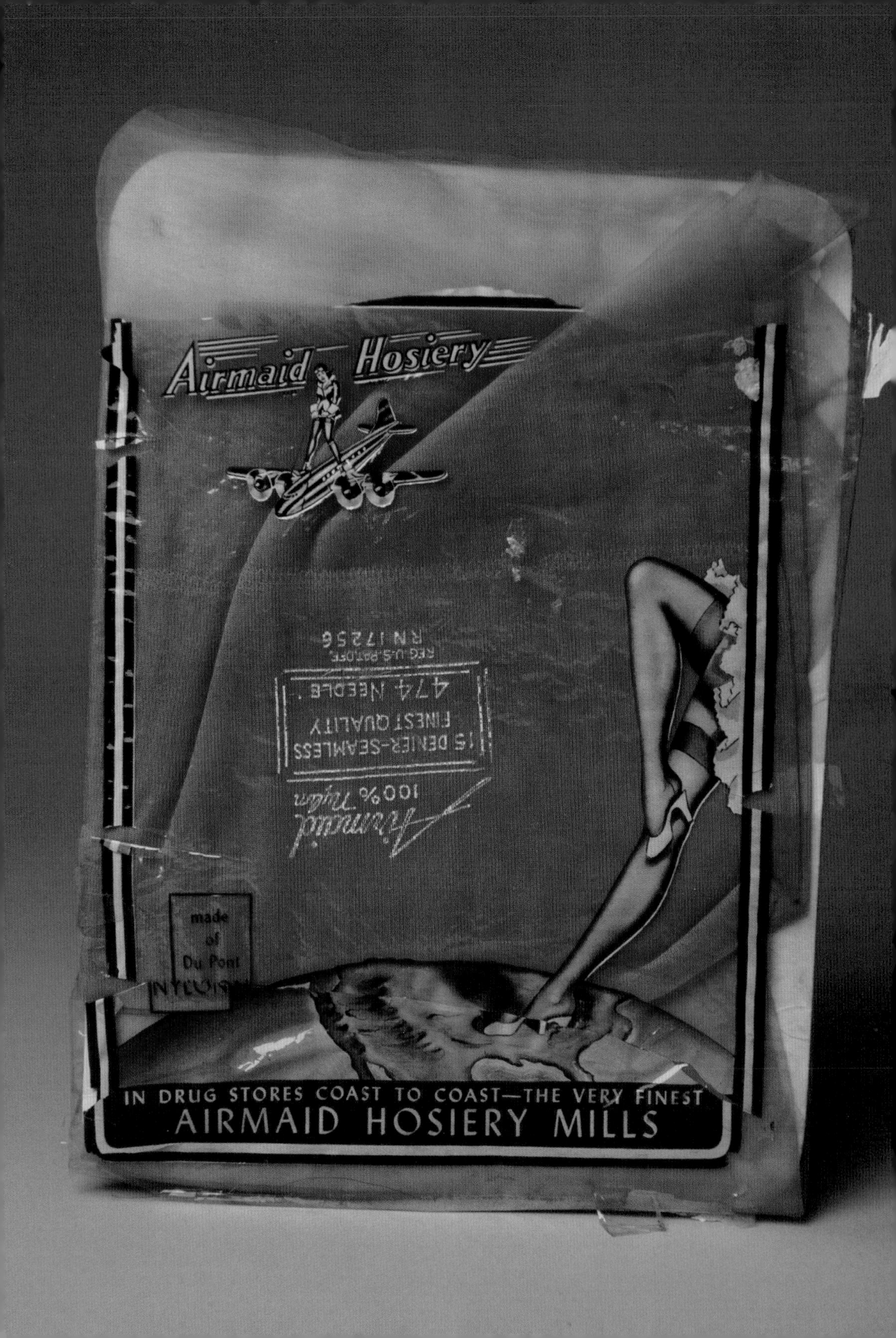
Airmaid Hosiery
made of Du Pont NYLON
IN DRUG STORES COAST TO COAST—THE VERY FINEST
AIRMAID HOSIERY MILLS

Tips from the *National Airlines Stewardess Flight Manual,* 1980

On Conduct

The conduct of a Flight Attendant is always under the surveillance of her passengers. Your attitude, appearance, and behavior reflects upon the airline and your fellow employees.

Passengers expect a Flight Attendant to be polite, respectful, considerate, and attentive. If you fail to meet their expectations, they will consider not only you, but the entire flight a disappointment.

Remember, the impressions you leave with your passengers may determine whether they fly with us again, or choose another airline.

As a Flight Attendant, you will enjoy a career that you will remember all your life and for that reason, it deserves no less than your best.

On Grooming

The Flight Attendant's complexion should be kept at its best.

Cosmetics must harmonize with skin tone. Eye make-up should appear natural. Refrain from repairing make-up in view of passengers.

Hands and fingernails shall be maintained in a clean and well-manicured condition, as they are in constant view of the public. Nails shall be evenly shaped, moderate in length, polished or well buffed for a glossy appearance. Polish shades shall be complimentary to the uniform color.

Hair should be neat and attractively styled to complement facial structure and give a professional appearance. Hair cannot be longer than the top of the shoulder in front, or longer than the top of the shoulder blade in back. Hair coloring is permitted provided it is complimentary to the overall appearance of the individual. Color must be maintained in a natural tone.

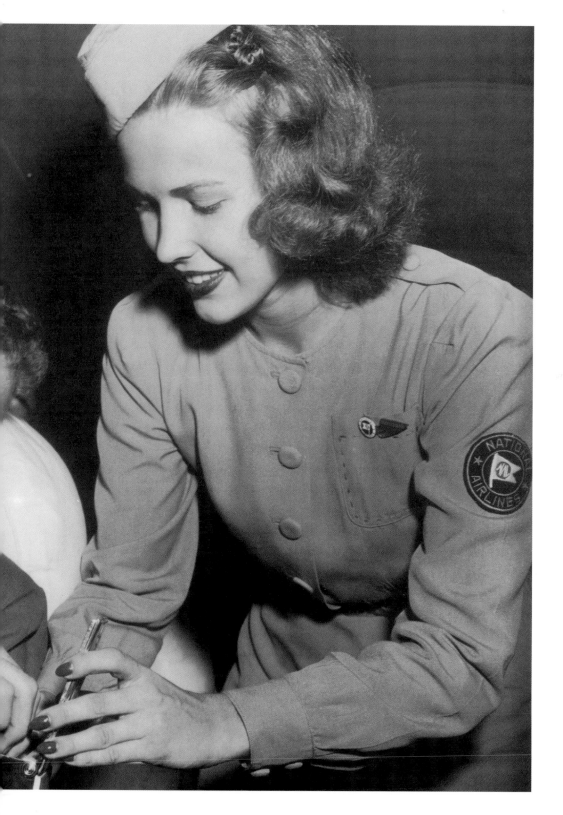

Stewardess Creed

If you who enter here have come sincerely
    And know exactly where your interest lies,
Have tired of office job, school, or nursing—
    Yet thrilled to the flash of silver in the skies;
If you have longed to see our nation's beauty
    Not limited to the east or western shore,
Can love all people, knowing each can teach you
    And make you bigger than you were before;
If you have learned to sympathize with sorrow,
    Open your heart to everyone you greet—
And if you honestly respect the culture
    Of any creed or color you may meet;
If you have patience born of understanding,
    And pride not lessened though the task be small;
If you can gain the joy from helping others,
    And have the will to give this job your all;
If you have loyalty unswayed by cynics,
    Put kindness far above your own demands,
Can realize all aviation's problems
    But aid the vision of its future plans—
Then you will know this miracle of flying,
    The comradeship, the progress, and what's more—
You'll feel the very pulse beat of our country.
    Welcome to the Stewardess Corps.

Ground and flight personnel will represent the new Pan Am in stylishly professional new uniforms. Flight attendants are outfitted by Adolfo in a choice of Pan Am Blue (far left) or navy, with camel accents and optional hats. Cacharel's creations for Ground Passenger Services are available in navy and Cacharel Blue (second from right), accented by blouses in fuchsia or blue. Models are (left to right) Flight Attendants Christina Shull, Joel Jacobs and Shelley Hall; Ground Passenger Services Representatives Richard Keim, Lousia Anthony and Margarita Subiros.

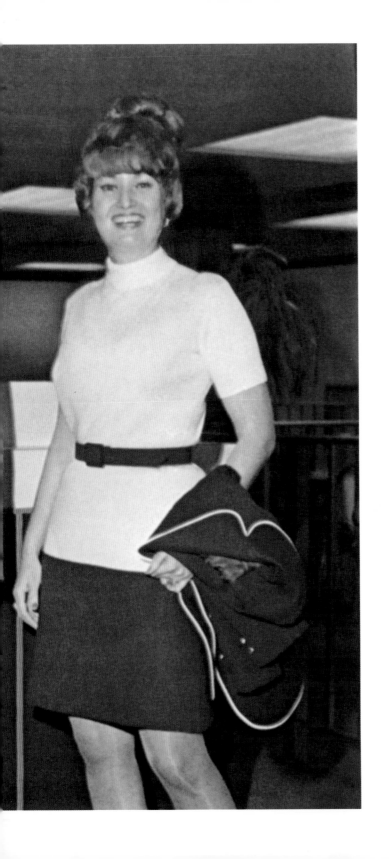

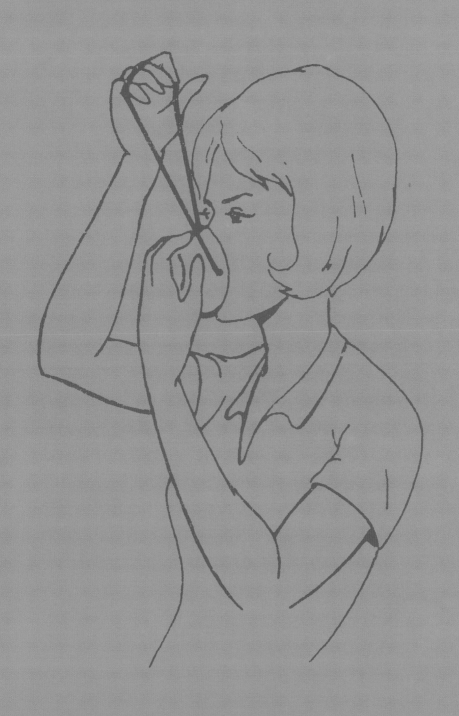

1 MOVIE SOUNDTRACK

3 THE CLASSICS

Vittorino Respighi	The Fountains of Rome Charles Munch Conducting The New Philharmonia Orchestra	London SPC-21024
Ferdi Grofé	Grand Canyon Suite The London Festival Orchestra Conducted By Stanley Black	London SPC-21002
Johann Strauss	The Emperor Waltz The Vienna Philharmonic Orchestra Josef Krips Conducting	London STS-15012

4 STEREO NOW

The Sound of Sight with Ray Martin	Overture To End All Overtures Destination Space Tearjerker Whodunnit	London Phase 4 SP-44040
Enoch Light and The Light Brigade	Far Away Places Provocative Percussion	Command RS 821 SD
The Young Americans	Little Joy On The Blue Cloud Sea	ABC S-659
Through The Looking Glass with Lionel Bart	THE FINDER Isn't This Where We Came In? Looking Glass, Looking Glass May A Man Be Merry? Throw Away Collapsible Soapbox	Deram DES 18020
The World's Greatest Jazz Band	Alfie	PR 5039 SD
Trooping The Colour with The Band of the Brenadier Guards	The Duke of York March Lillibulero Money Music Royal Birthday	London Phase 4 SP-44040

5 POTPOURRI

The Young Americans	Born To Be With You	ABC S-586
Anita Kerr & The Anita Kerr Singers	Wine In The Wind	Warner Bros.- 7 Arts WS-1750
The Ray Charles Singers	1432 Franklin Pike Circle Hero	Command 942S
The Wonderful World of Antonio Carlos Jobim	Dindi	Warner Bros.- 7 Arts WS-1611
One of Those Songs – Jimmy Durante	Old Man Time	Warner Bros.- 7 Arts WS-1655
Theodore Bikel	I Hear The Laughter	Reprise 6348
Sammy Davis, Jr. and Laurindo Almeida, guitarist	Two Different Worlds	Reprise 6236
Anna & Frederick Sing In French	Mes Enfants	MLP 15255
Diahann Carroll	Blah Blah Blah	Atlantic 8048
Kay Starr with Count Basie	Goodtime Girl	Paramount PAS 5001
Anna & Frederick Sing In French	Pourquoi J'aime Paris	MLP 15276
Charles Aznavour Sings In French	Le Temps	Reprise R-6172
Orietta Berti	Fior de Bambu (Raddish Leaves)	London International TW 91418
Sammy Davis, Jr.	In This Crowded World	Reprise RS 6339
Charles Aznavour Sings In Spanish	Buen Aniversario	Monument SLP 18098
Tom Jones	Polk Salad Annie	Parrot XPAS 71037
Jimmy Durante	What Became Of Life	Warner Bros.- 7 Arts W-1655
The Young Americans	Goodbye Sadness	ABC S-586

6 MOOD MUSIC

Mantovani	Love Makes The World Go Round	London PS 119
The 101 Strings	Where Is Love	Alshire S-5149
The David Whitaker Orchestra	The Lonely One	Deram SML 13703
Hugo Winterhalter & His Orchestra	You're Nobody Till Somebody Loves You	Musicor M2S-3168
The 101 Strings	Love Is Worth Waiting For	Alshire S-5005
The 101 Strings	I'm A Man	Alshire S-5078
The Sears Golden Strings	Love Walked In	Sears SPS-206
Jackie Gleason & His Orchestra	I Remember You	Pickwick PTP2004
The 101 Strings	Where Or When	Alshire S-5009
The 101 Strings	If I Loved You	Alshire S-5010
Jackie Gleason & His Orchestra	You Were Meant For Me	Pickwick PTP 2004
Enoch Light & The Brass Menagerie	I'm Gonna Make You Love Me	Project Three PR 5036S1
Gordon Franks & His Orchestra	Love In The Open Air	Deram SML 13701
Boots Randolph With Strings	You've Lost That Lovin' Feelin'	Monument SLP 18066
Mantovani	Games That Lovers Play	London LL 3483
Mantovani	Smoke Gets In Your Eyes	London PS 542
Doc Severensen & Friends	Goin' Out Of My Head	Command RS 909S
The 101 Strings	If Ever I Would Leave You	Alshire S-5014
Enoch Light & The Brass Menagerie	The Fool On The Hill	Project Three PR 50365
The 101 Strings	A Woman Is A Sometime Thing	Alshire S-5006

7 DISCOTHEQUE

Reincarnation	Reincarnation You Look Like A Memory City Cat	ABC Probe CPLP-4508
The Outlaw Blues Band	Tobacco Road Lost In The Blues	Bluesway BLS-6021
Marianne Faithfull	As Tears Go By Is This What I Get For Loving You	London PS-547
The Electric Prunes	Giant Sunhorse	Reprise 6342
Silk	Scottish Thing For All Time	ABC S-694
B. B. King	The Thrill Is Gone Confessin' The Blues	Bluesway BLS-6037
Wings	That's Not Real Generation Breakdown	Dunhill DS-50046
	Cloudy Summer Afternoon There's Nothing Else On My Mind	Dunhill DS-50033

8 JAZZ

Thad Jones and Mel Lewis	Live At The Village Vanguard Li Willow Tree Bacha Feelin'	SS-18016
Buddy Rich	Swingin' New Big Band Sister Sadie More Soul Westside Story Medley	PJ-10113
Quincy Jones	Walking In Space Dead End Walking In Space	A & M SP-3023

Some airlines have special equipment and toys for youngsters.

SECRET OF AIRLINE SERVICE
UNIQUE IN ALL THE WORLD

As part of your Olympic holiday in Japan plan now to enjoy a travel experience unique in all the world. The enchantment of Japan begins the moment your JAL hostess welcomes you aboard a magnificent Japan Air Lines Jet Courier, bound for the pagentry of the XVIII Olympiad.

Your hostess has been trained from childhood to please her guests in the classic Japanese manner. Her kimono-clad grace, as she attends your every wish, is delightfully complemented by the cabin decor.....a decor reminicent of a classic Japanese home.

Plan now to come early and to stay on in Japan following the games. You'll find the fall one of the most beautiful times of the year in Japan. Or if you are making a round-the-world trip or journey to Hong Kong or Bangkok see your travel agent or Japan Air Lines.

A "regular" BOAC tunic...a slit-skirt cheong sam...a sari

"We'll see you around...the globe!"

"We are all wearing uniforms of the BOAC Stewardesses you meet in different parts of the world.

"We serve your fellow-passengers from Bangkok, Hong Kong, Africa, from all 6 continents, in fact.

"If you're flying our route from Tokyo to London, it's very likely that a Stewardess will board your aircraft at Karachi, clad in a *sari*. It seems more homelike to a passenger from India or Pakistan, as she serves him the hot curry of his country.

"Whether we're Chinese or Indian or Scottish, we all fly to London for training right along with BOAC's future Stewards. Our course takes 8 to 10 weeks, with special coaching extra. It takes a lot of study to perform all the duties that are expected of us. British cabin service means individual attention to each passenger. No other airline's Stewardesses can provide it."

Equipment: BOAC flies you in the most modern aircraft, including "DC-7C's", jet-prop "Britannias" and pure jet "Comet 4's".

Classes of Fares...BOAC tickets cost exactly the same as those of other scheduled airlines. Round-trip, New York to London, they are de Luxe $900, First Class $792, Tourist $576, Economy $462.60.

Travel Agents' requests for your reservations are honored at all BOAC offices. They can give you travel and tour literature, time-tables and answers to your individual questions.

B·O·A·C

BRITISH OVERSEAS AIRWAYS CORPORATION
**THE MOST EXPERIENCED _JET_ AIRLINE
IN THE WORLD**

Flights from New York, Boston, Chicago, Detroit, Honolulu, San Francisco, Montreal. Offices also in Atlanta, Dallas, Los Angeles, Miami, Philadelphia, Pittsburgh, Washington, Toronto, Vancouver, Winnipeg.

TWA introduces "Foreign Accent" flights inside USA

Announcing the end of routine air travel: Now, when you
fly non-stop from New York or Chicago to California
(or back), you can fly one of our new "Foreign Accent" flights!

They come in four styles with hostesses to match: Italian (see toga),
French (see gold mini), Olde English (see wench). And Manhattan Penthouse
(see hostess pajamas—after all, hostesses should look like hostesses, right?)

You'll find a whole new atmosphere throughout the plane,
first-class and coach. Foreign music. Foreign magazines and newspapers.
Foreign touches all around. And the best in foreign cuisine.
(Yes, you may still enjoy a steak cooked to order. That's a TWA specialty).

All in all, TWA's new "Foreign Accent" flights bring you
the best the world has to offer. And if you're as bored with routine flying
as we think you are, you're ready for it.

Call us, or Mr. Information (your travel agent).
He knows all about it.

P.S. Get ready in Philadelphia, Washington,
Baltimore and Boston. "Foreign Accent"
flights coming soon.

up up and away* **TWA**

I'm Laura.
I've got daily 747's from Miami to Europe.

Fly me.

Starting May 25th I'll have more going for you to Europe than anyone else. With daily 747's to London, and great connections on to the great places in Europe.

I've got the nice convenience of 747's every day to London. And the added convenience of the Miami gateway, avoiding the congested northern airports.

I've got the beautiful luxury of the great 747 with more cabin room than any airliner in the sky today.

And I've got the 747 extras en route: first-run movies,* multi-channelled audio entertainment, and our international gourmet cuisine.

Give it a go, won't you? Fly me to London.

Telephone National direct, or ring up your travel agent. Tell him Laura sent you.

SAN FRANCISCO
OAKLAND/SAN JOSE

LOS A
O
LONG

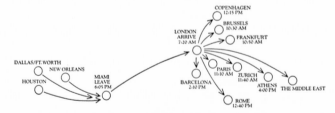

COPENHAGEN
12:15 PM

BRUSSELS
10:30 AM

LONDON
ARRIVE
7:20 AM

FRANKFURT
10:50 AM

DALLAS/FT. WORTH

NEW ORLEANS

PARIS
11:10 AM

ZURICH
11:40 AM

HOUSTON

MIAMI
LEAVE
6:05 PM

BARCELONA
2:10 PM

ATHENS
4:00 PM   THE MIDDLE EAST

ROME
12:40 PM

Fly Laura. Fly National.

going to fly you
e you've never
n flown before.

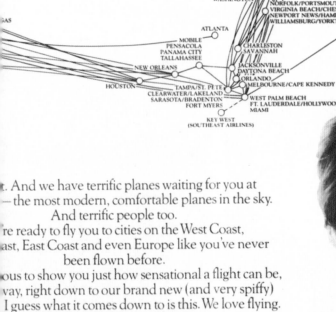

LONDON

BOSTON
PROVIDENCE

NEW YORK
NEWARK
PHILADELPHIA

BALTIMORE
WASHINGTON

NORFOLK/PORTSMOUTH
VIRGINIA BEACH/CHESAPEAKE
NEWPORT NEWS/HAMPTON
WILLIAMSBURG/YORKTOWN

GAS

ATLANTA

MOBILE
PENSACOLA
PANAMA CITY
TALLAHASSEE

CHARLESTON
SAVANNAH

NEW ORLEANS

JACKSONVILLE
DAYTONA BEACH
ORLANDO
MELBOURNE/CAPE KENNEDY

HOUSTON

TAMPA/ST. PETE
CLEARWATER/LAKELAND
SARASOTA/BRADENTON
FORT MYERS

WEST PALM BEACH
FT. LAUDERDALE/HOLLYWOOD
MIAMI

KEY WEST
(SOUTHEAST AIRLINES)

t. And we have terrific planes waiting for you at
— the most modern, comfortable planes in the sky.
And terrific people too.
re ready to fly you to cities on the West Coast,
ast, East Coast and even Europe like you've never
been flown before.
ous to show you just how sensational a flight can be,
ay, right down to our brand new (and very spiffy)
I guess what it comes down to is this. We love flying.
And we want you to love flying us.

your travel agent.
National.

BUIA
BRITISH UNITED ISLAND AIRWAYS

SUMMER TIMETABLE
valid from 1st Apr. until 31st Oct. 1969

Subject to alteration without notice

EAGLE
SUPER-VISCOUNT 805
TO
BERMUDA
AND
NASSAU
THE ONLY ALL JET-POWERED SERVICE

Britain's
Largest
Independent
Scheduled
Airline

IRAN AIR
هواپیمایی ملی ایران » هما «

SOMMERFLUGPLAN 1974
Gültig: vom 1. Juli 1974 bis 31. Oktober 1974
(IATA-Mitglied)

Kom fort med
KAR·AIR

Philippine
Airlines
INTERNATIONAL WINTER TIMETABLE
EFFECTIVE NOVEMBER 1, 1971 TO MARCH 31, 1972

AVIANCA
THE COLOMBIAN AIRLINE
NORTH · CENTRAL · SOUTH AMERICA AND EUROPE

TIMETABLE

FIRST AIRLINE IN THE AMERICAS

ITINERARIOS   VIGENCIA: 1.º ABRIL 1969

AVIANCA
La Linea Aérea Internacional Colombiana

SUR
CENTRO
NORTEAMERICA
Y
EUROPA

AGENTES GENERALES: PAN AMERICAN WORLD AIRWAYS

CAMBRIAN
BRITISH AIR SERVICES

Summer Timetable
1st April to 31st October 1970

BRITISH
CALEDONIAN

system timetable

WINTER 1971/2
Valid from 1st November until 31st March
SUBJECT TO ALTERATION WITHOUT NOTICE

ALASKA   # ALASKA
AIRLINES

GOLDEN
SAMOVAR
SERVICE

SUMMER   1970
TIMETABLE

GOLDEN
SAMOVAR
SERVICE

EFFECTIVE JANUARY 1, 1941

CHICAGO & SOUTHERN

CHICAGO - ST. LOUIS - MEMPHIS - JACKSON -
NEW ORLEANS

DIXIE LINER
SERVICE

C&S

IT PAYS TO *FLY*

Effective October 1, 1966

DELTA
AIR LINES

Jet Delta...
nicest way
to eat up
600 miles

TIME TABLE FOLDER
EFFECTIVE NOVEMBER 1, 1944
Containing Fares and Interline Connections

BRANIFF
Airways

IT'S *Still*
FRIENDLY TRANSPORTATION

FROM THE GREAT *Lakes*...
and the Rockies
...TO THE GULF

CAL-STATE AIR LINES
WE'VE GOT CONNECTIONS
Flight Schedule Effective September 1, 1969

TAA
timetable

Olympic Games
Melbourne
22nd November — 8th December

effective from
17th November
1956

TRANS-AUSTRALIA AIRLINES

Effective **OCTOBER 1, 1939**

TWA

The Airline Run by Flyers

TRANSCONTINENTAL
& WESTERN AIR, Inc.
Shortest..Fastest..Coast to Coast

BWIA
CARIBBEAN TIMETABLE

Effective
APRIL 28, 1968
UNTIL FURTHER NOTICE

LIAT
AIR JAMAICA
JAMAICA AIR SERVICE

NEW YORK
MONTREAL
BURLINGTON

CANADIAN COLONIAL AIRWAYS

CANADIAN
COLONIAL
AIRWAYS
Be there rather than On Your Way

CCA

AIR FRANCE

Horaires d'Été
Summer Timetables   N° 3   Sommer-Flugplan
Horarios de Verano

15. 5. 70 — 30. 6. 70

Prochaine Edition : *Next Issue :* Nächste Ausgabe : *Proxima Edicion :*
1.7.70

AIR FRANCE

N° 6

EDITION DU 1ᵉʳ SEPT. - PROCHAINE EDITION 1ᵉʳ NOV.

EDITION 1ˢᵗ SEPT. - NEXT ISSUE 1ˢᵗ NOV.

INDICATEUR GENERAL	FLUGPLAN
ÉTÉ : 1ᵉʳ Avril - 31 Octobre	SOMMER : 1. April - 31. Oktober
GENERAL TIME TABLE	HORARIOS Y TARIFAS
SUMMER : 1ˢᵗ April - 31ˢᵗ October	VERANO : 1 de Abril - 31 de Octubre

1966

AIR FRANCE

1966

Édition du 15 Mai
Prochaine édition : 28 Juin

Edition 15th May
Next issue : 28th June

n° 4

indicateur général
ÉTÉ - 1ᵉʳ Avril - 31 Octobre

general time table
SUMMER - 1ˢᵗ April - 31ˢᵗ October

flugplan
SOMMER - 1. April - 31. Oktober

horarios y tarifas
VERANO - 1 de Abril - 31 de Octubre

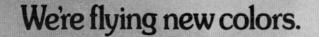

We're flying new colors.

6 cheerful colors. In dresses that make our stewardesses feel even more feminine than before. And more eager than ever to spread cheer around our airplanes.

We have new ground colors, too. For the hostesses who help you out in our terminals. But new colors are only part of what we're doing at Eastern to make flying more enjoyable for everyone.

Come take a look. We'll welcome you smiling. And we'll do all we can to see that you leave us that way.

EASTERN. Smiling faces going places.

now*...
BRANIFF
serves
MEXICO
direct
with
famed

Silver
Service.

flights

Braniff has captured the festive spirit of Mexico with Silver Service . . . the most lavish service on either side of the Border. You'll enjoy vintage champagne . . . a wide selection of other beverages . . . melt-in-your-mouth hors d'oeuvres served with a flair from the serving cart. Relax, if you wish, in the spacious lounge. Thoughtful extras make Braniff's famed Silver Service an unrivaled adventure in travel elegance . . . at no extra fare! Direct one-plane service between the U. S. A. and Mexico City. Both first class and tourist. Fly now—pay later. Ask your travel agent about the many tours available or call

Acapulco
MEXICO CITY

BRANIFF
International
AIRWAYS

Braniff serves more major cities in the U. S. A. and Latin America than any other airline.

*Starts November 9th

WING YOUR WAY WITH...

AUSTRALIAN NATIONAL AIRWAYS
ANA

FROM NORTH TO SOUTH AMERICA . . .
FROM NEW YORK TO JAMAICA . . .
FROM SOUTH AMERICA TO EUROPE
VIA PUERTO RICO

Star Studded Routes

TO ROMANTIC PLACES

A smile from that charming hostess in the red ruana* . . .
sleek luxury to delight you aboard Super Constellations that
fly a million passengers a year . . . your meals
prepared by a famous New York chef, wines and liqueurs
of mellow perfection . . . the hospitality and efficiency
of a great international airline.

AVIANCA. Oldest Airline in the Americas, for 38 years
a leader among the passenger air fleets of the world . . .
largest air freight carrier under any flag.

* NEW YORK
* MIAMI   PARIS * FRANKFURT
* JAMAICA   MADRID
                                     * LISBON
PANAMA *   * PUERTO RICO   AZORES
BOGOTA   * CARACAS
* QUITO
* LIMA

*Smart modern version of
the red woolen cloak from
Colombian Andes, now
proudly displayed by
AVIANCA hostesses.

SEE YOUR TRAVEL AGENT

AVIANCA
OLDEST AIRLINE IN THE AMERICAS
COLOMBIAN NATIONAL AIRWAYS

PAN AMERICAN
General Agents

Grace Downs

AIR CAREER SCHOOL

FOR GIRLS WHO LIKE ADVENTURE AND TRAVEL *plus* A FINE SALARY

BE AN AIRLINE HOSTESS

"FLY JET"—for Pay!
Greet on-coming passengers at lunch time in New York and say farewell before dinner in California. . . . **FREE** life-time placement service by Grace Downs.

RAPID CO-ED COURSE
Experienced airline executives teach you in Day and Evening Classes in the school's own 48 passenger cabin plane and in the Link Trainer which simulates flying. Amphitheatres, study halls, large classrooms in block long fireproof school building, within walking distance of the United Nations Building and Eastside Airline Terminal.

BE AN AIRLINE SECRETARY

If higher education is your goal . . . then consider this program
GRACE DOWNS "Three in One" course:

1. **Complete Secretarial**—Gregg shorthand, speed typing, teletype, public speaking, English, diction, vocabulary on college level, reception work, office practices, etc.

2. **Complete Air Hostess**—ticketing, reservations course. Take dictation in the terminology of the Air Age. Airline executives must have secretaries who know routes, codes, scheduling, types of aircraft, etc.

3. **The Complete Model Course**—for your self-improvement or free lance modeling to supplement your income.

For the Jet Age, Airlines are hiring Secretaries, Executives, Passenger Agents, Reservationists, Hostesses. With previous typing and shorthand you enter advanced course and save time. **New** prestige careers offer rapid promotions, high pay, adventure and travel. **Meet** interesting and important people who Air Travel while you work on the ground or in the air.

This 2 year program can be completed in one year with the usual college vacations. The Grace Downs method is rapid, thorough—intensive but condensed—includes all 3 courses.

BE A MODEL—OR LOOK LIKE ONE

New York's oldest model school trains you for high salaried positions in Television, Fashion, Photography and Motion Pictures. Day or evening courses. **FREE** placement service. Take this separately or in combination with the above one or two courses!

SUPERVISED DORMITORIES IN SCHOOL BUILDING

Licensed by New York State Department of Education
Accredited by the world's leading airlines.
ESTABLISHED 1927

Since 1945 Grace Downs has personally conducted the Miss New York City Pageant

Theresa Silk
Stewardess Capital Airlin
(A Grace Downs Gradua

Olive Guyton
Airline Flight and Ground See
Ayres, Inc., Park Avenue, N.
(A Grace Downs Graduat

Louise Bayka
Now—Popular Teacher and M
(A Grace Downs Graduat

Grace Downs

NEW YORK UNIVERSITY BUILDING

477 FIRST AVE. at 28th ST., NEW YORK 16, N. Y. • ORegon 9-6440

WRITE DEPT. MA FOR FULL INFORMATION

NATIONAL'S COAST TO COAST TO COAST
CUT-OUTS

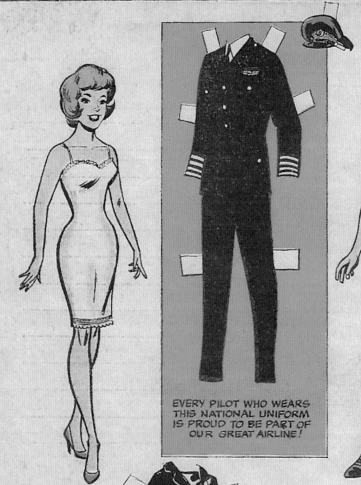

EVERY PILOT WHO WEARS THIS NATIONAL UNIFORM IS PROUD TO BE PART OF OUR GREAT AIRLINE!

HERE IS NATIONAL'S HIGH-FASHION STEWARDESS UNIFORM DESIGNED BY CASSINI! IT'S MADE OF IMPORTED MOHAIR TO ADAPT TO A WIDE RANGE OF TEMPERATURES, SINCE NATIONAL JETS FROM NEW YORK AND BOSTON TO MIAMI AND FROM FLORIDA TO CALIFORNIA!

THE WHITE BERET IS MADE OF THE FINEST CALFSKIN; GLOVES ARE KID!

16

FIND THE TWINS!

THERE ARE *TWO* SETS OF TWINS FLYING ON NATIONAL AIRLINES! LOOK AT ALL THE PRETTY STEWARDESSES BELOW AND SEE IF YOU CAN FIND THE *TWO PAIRS* OF *TWINS!*

12.

ACK

ACKNOWLEDGMENTS

There were many who graciously shared their experiences and memories of life in the sky with me. My thanks and gratitude to Vicki Nicely, whose box of memorabilia showed me how unique this book could be. To the National Sundowners (Mary Daniel, Judith Howard, Suzanne Crawford Johnson, Linda Marcrum, Kay Strauss), whose enthusiasm, support, photos, and scrapbooks were priceless—I wish I could go back in time and fly with you. Thanks to Tom Bailey, Ron Dawson, David Henderson, Ken Jensen, Chris Laborde of jetPSA.com, Bjorn Larsson, Trina Robbins, and Donald West for allowing me to showcase items from their collections. To Steve Mockus, Tera Killip, and everyone at Chronicle Books, for making this project happen. To Ben Shaykin, yet again, for his beautiful design. And always, to Jon, Isabel, and Jack—my flight crew.

Ladies and gentlemen, we are making our final

approach into _____.

Please recheck that your seat belts are securely

fastened, place your seats and tray tables in the

upright position, and observe the "No Smoking"

and seat-belt signs.

If you have used any carry-on articles during

the flight, please be sure that they are properly

stowed for landing. Thank you for flying with us.

Thank you. Have a nice day. Thank you. Have a nic